D0502023

Prescott Public Library
Prescott, Arizona

Needs and Wants

by Gillia M. Olson
Consulting Editor: Gail Saunders-Smith, PhD

Consultant: Sharon M. Danes, PhD
Professor and Family Economist
University of Minnesota

Capstone
press.

Mankato, Minnesota

Pebble Books are published by Capstone Press,
151 Good Counsel Drive, P.O. Box 669, Mankato, Minnesota 56002.
www.capstonepress.com

Copyright © 2009 by Capstone Press, a Capstone Publishers company.
All rights reserved.
No part of this publication may be reproduced in whole or in part,
or stored in a retrieval system, or transmitted in any form or by any means,
electronic, mechanical, photocopying, recording, or otherwise,
without written permission of the publisher.
For information regarding permission, write to Capstone Press,
151 Good Counsel Drive, P.O. Box 669, Dept. R, Mankato, Minnesota 56002.
Printed in the United States of America

1 2 3 4 5 6 13 12 11 10 09 08

Library of Congress Cataloging-in-Publication Data
Olson, Gillia M.
    Needs and wants / by Gillia M. Olson.
    p. cm.
    Includes bibliographical references and index.
    ISBN-13: 978-1-4296-1707-9 (hardcover)
    ISBN-10: 1-4296-1707-1 (hardcover)
    1. Need (Psychology) — Juvenile literature. 2. Desire — Juvenile literature.
    I. Title.
BF723.N44O47 2009
153.8 — dc22   2008001207

Summary: Describes the concept of needs and wants and making choices between
    the two.

Note to Parents and Teachers

Needs and Wants supports national economics standards. The
images support early readers in understanding the text. The
repetition of words and phrases helps early readers learn new
words. This book also introduces early readers to subject-specific
vocabulary words, which are defined in the Glossary section. Early
readers may need assistance to read some words and to use the
Table of Contents, Glossary, Read More, Internet Sites, and Index
sections of the book.

Table of Contents

4

What Are Needs and Wants?

Needs are the things
we must have to live.
Food, clothing, and
a place to live are needs.

Wants are things
we can live without.
Bicycles, toys, and movies
are wants.

Telling Them Apart

Needs and wants can be
hard to tell apart.
Soda is something Peter wants.
Water is something he needs.

Emily needs a warm coat.
It doesn't have to be new.
Emily's sister gives her
a coat she has outgrown.

Making Choices

Peter's family makes choices with their money. First, all family members must have their needs met.

A family may have money
left over to use for wants.
Peter's family is able
to meet all its needs
plus some wants.

Peter got some money
for his birthday.
He can buy something
he wants.

Peter wants a movie
and a video game.
He doesn't have
enough money for both.
He makes a choice.

Peter gives up one thing
to have the other.
What would you do?

Glossary

choice — the chance to pick one thing over another

need — something you must have to live

outgrow — to grow too big for something

video game — a game played on a television or computer screen by using buttons or levers

want — something you would like to have but can live without

Read More

Firestone, Mary. *Spending Money.* First Facts: Learning about Money. Mankato, Minn.: Capstone Press, 2005.

Ring, Susan. *Needs and Wants.* Mankato, Minn.: Yellow Umbrella Books, 2003.

Internet Sites

FactHound offers a safe, fun way to find Internet sites related to this book. All of the sites on FactHound have been researched by our staff.

Here's how:

1. Visit *www.facthound.com*
2. Choose your grade level.
3. Type in this book ID **1429617071** for age-appropriate sites. You may also browse subjects by clicking on letters, or by clicking on pictures and words.
4. Click on the **Fetch It** button.

FactHound will fetch the best sites for you!   23

Index

Word Count: 154
Grade: 1
Early-Intervention Level: *14*

Editorial Credits
Erika L. Shores, editor; Renée T. Doyle, designer;
   Sarah L. Schuette, photo stylist; Marcy Morin, scheduler

Photo Credits
Capstone Press/Karon Dubke, all

The author dedicates this book to her inspiration, Doug.